·S·M·O·K·I·N·G·

Anne Charlish

Points of View

Abortion
Advertising
Alcohol
Animal Rights
Apartheid
Capital Punishment
Censorship
Divorce
Drugs
Medical Ethics
Northern Ireland
Nuclear Weapons
Racism
Sex and Sexuality
Smoking
Terrorism

Front cover: *A dangerous habit, or one of life's little pleasures? Smoking is presently at the centre of a major public debate.*

Editors: William Wharfe/Marcella Streets
Designer: David Armitage

First published in 1990 by
Wayland (Publishers) Limited
61 Western Road, Hove
East Sussex BN3 1JD, England

© Copyright 1990 Wayland (Publishers) Limited

British Library Cataloguing in Publication Data
Charlish, Anne
  Smoking — (Points of view).
  1. Tobacco smoking. Social aspects.
  I. Title. II. Series.
  306'.4

ISBN 1-85210-843-6

Phototypeset by Direct Image Photosetting Ltd,
Hove, East Sussex, England
Printed in Italy by G. Canale & C.S.p.A., Turin
Bound in France by A.G.M.

Author's note
First of all, I should like to thank Dr John Cutting (Consultant Psychiatrist, Bethlem Royal and Maudsley Hospitals) without whose calm support and practical assistance I might never have emerged from the avalanche of material that research into smoking inevitably produces.

I should also like to thank the following for their kind assistance: Liz Batten, Director of Smokestop and Senior Research Fellow in the Department of Psychology, University of Southampton; Michael Belcher, Clinical Nurse Specialist, Smokers Clinic, The Maudsley Hospital, London; Dr Anne Charlton, Director of Cancer Research Campaign Education and Child Studies Research Group, University of Manchester; Dr Bobbie Jacobson, Physician, Department of Community Medicine, St Leonard's Hospital, London; Martin Jarvis, Senior Lecturer and Clinical Psychologist, Imperial Cancer Research Fund, Health Behaviour Unit, Institute of Psychiatry, London; Dr Ann McNeill, Research Psychologist, Addiction Research Unit, The Institute of Psychiatry, London; W J Owen, Consultant Surgeon, Guy's Hospital, London; Dr Frances Parrish, General Practitioner, Sussex; Dr Federico G Puente Silva, Consultant Psychiatrist and President of COMECTA, the Mexican Committee for the Study and Control of Smoking, Mexico City; Dr Michael Russell, Consultant Psychiatrist, Addiction Research Unit, The Institute of Psychiatry, London; David Simpson, Director of Action on Smoking and Health (ASH); Ann Siswell, Senior Information Officer, Action on Smoking and Health (ASH); Dr Chris Steele, ITV's *This Morning*'s family doctor, Manchester general practitioner and director of SmokeQuitters stop-smoking clinics; Janet Thornley, and her pupils, Notre Dame School, Lingfield, Surrey.

I owe a special debt of gratitude to Peter Taylor for his compelling book, *The Smoke Ring: Tobacco, Money and Multinational Politics*.

Lastly, I should like to thank those organizations quoted in the text and those listed at the back of this book who were kind enough to assist me.

*Note on quotations from FOREST publications on page 26. FOREST has asked the publishers to point out that 'FOREST does not supply its information to those under the age of eighteen as it believes that only adults have the right to choose on this sensitive issue'.

Contents

1	Introduction	4
2	Why people smoke	8
3	'I'm dying for a cigarette'	17
4	'It's my life, isn't it?'	24
5	Giving up	36
6	The future	41
7	Conclusion	44

Glossary	46
Further information	46
Further reading	47
Index	48

Introduction

> What difference is there between a smoker and a suicide; except that the one takes longer to kill himself than the other? (Jacob Balde, Jesuit priest, 1658.)

Over 300 years later, the same connection can still be made:

> Smokers take in over 3,000 harmful substances. The main ones are tar, carbon monoxide, nicotine, and cyanide and its derivatives. It's slow-motion suicide, as Joe Califano, American Secretary for Health, Education and Welfare, said over a decade ago. You're killing yourself slowly. (Dr Chris Steele, family doctor on ITV's *This Morning*, Manchester GP and director of SmokeQuitters stop-smoking clinics, 1989.)

A humorous painting depicts the moment when Sir Walter Raleigh (1552–1618), one of the first Europeans to discover tobacco, had his first smoke. Tobacco smoking soon became popular throughout Europe.

People will satisfy their addiction to nicotine, once it has taken hold, even if it means there is less money for essentials such as food, housing and clothing. Here in Mexico, tobacco is very big business.

Cigarette smoking causes 100,000 premature deaths a year in Britain, 23,000 premature deaths in Australia every year and some 350,000 annually in the USA. All over the world people are dying before their time because of smoking. Few smokers can claim ignorance of the medical hazards of smoking: most developed countries of the world insist that every packet of cigarettes carries some sort of health warning. So why do people continue to smoke? Why do they slowly kill themselves?

The aim of this book is to identify the reasons for this surprising behaviour. The reasons are complex. The essential problem is one of individual addiction. This book looks at the reasons why an individual becomes addicted, remains addicted and has great difficulty in giving up smoking. It examines the role of governments and tobacco companies which gain financially from people smoking. Meanwhile, in the developing countries, where food and medical supplies are in desperately short supply, 'business is booming' for the tobacco industry, as tycoon James Goldsmith noted in July 1989 during his bid for British American Tobacco.

> Tobacco consumption in Latin America has increased tremendously. We have 15 million people in the 15 to 19 age group in Mexico. They, and women [in general], constitute the target of the transnational tobacco companies ... US$80 million were spent on TV publicity in Mexico alone in 1988. In many developing countries, such as Mexico, the single tobacco producer is the government. They use cheap labour and they sell the tobacco to the transnational companies at a low price. (Dr Federico G Puente Silva, President of COMECTA, the Mexican Committee for the Study and Control of Smoking, 1989.)

Five trillion cigarettes are manufactured world-wide each year; 125 billion of these are produced in the UK.

British pubs are notoriously smoky. Few landlords have had the courage to provide non-smokers (two-thirds of the adult population) with a smoke-free environment. The exception pictured here is ahead of his time.

Smoking is not a rich person's luxury; conversely, it is often the poorest who smoke most. In most developed countries, more unskilled and semi-skilled workers smoke than those in the professions, and the latter are giving up faster. In the UK, more unemployed than employed people smoke: 50 per cent of the unemployed smoked in 1986, when overall, less than 35 per cent of adults smoked. Young, unemployed single mothers are one of the notable low-income groups that smoke the most.

Many people consider smoking to be antisocial in its risks and annoyance to others:

> Passive smoking is what happens to a non-smoker who is in a room with people who are smoking. Researchers have found that non-smokers who have been in the company of smokers have nicotine and increased levels of carbon monoxide in their blood, because the smoke that burns from the tip of a cigarette and has not been filtered is the most harmful part. The children of people who smoke get more chest infections than those whose parents don't smoke. (Mary Harrison, aged fourteen, in her project on smoking, at Notre Dame School, Lingfield, Surrey, 1989.)

Introduction

In most developed countries, smoking in public is increasingly being made illegal, for example on trains and buses, internal air flights, in shops, cinemas, theatres and a few restaurants. In the USA, some states — Minnesota being the first — have introduced a Clean Air Act, prohibiting smoking in enclosed public places, and stating that the non-smoker has the right to enjoy a smoke-free atmosphere. In Britain, however, there is no such Act, despite the fact that 67 per cent of adults are non-smokers or ex-smokers.

This book focuses on smoking cigarettes, but the smoking of tobacco in any form is harmful. Many former cigarette smokers turn to cigars, and because they have learned to inhale cigarette smoke, they continue to inhale when they smoke cigars. Four cigars are roughly equivalent to ten cigarettes; so a smoker of twenty small cigars a day may be inhaling more poisonous substances than when they were a cigarette smoker.

What does the smoker get from smoking? Is there a powerful force at play, something so powerful that it overrides normal concerns for one's health and consideration for others?

> Nicotine is certainly just as addictive as heroin and in fact it's just as hard to come off smoking tobacco as it is to come off heroin. (Dr Michael Russell, Addiction Research Unit, Institute of Psychiatry, London, in an interview with the author, 1989.)

In 1987 in the USA, more manual workers than professional workers smoked:

42.7 per cent of male manual workers smoked, compared with 21.5 per cent of male professional workers, and 37.8 per cent of female manual workers smoked, compared with 20 per cent of female professional workers (see also tables on page 45).

Nicotiana tabacum: *the tobacco plant. If its qualities and dangers had been fully understood when first discovered, it would never have been allowed on the market in the many forms we have now — cigarettes, cigars, pipe tobacco and chewing tobacco.*

Why people smoke

There are three phases in the development of a smoking habit: initiation (usually in childhood or in the early teens), enjoyment, and addiction or dependence. Major scientific studies have shown that children learn to inhale quite soon after initiation and experimentation with smoking, which means they are taking in nicotine. At this stage they enter the 'enjoyment' phase of smoking. The third stage, dependence, occurs shortly, almost always before the smoker is twenty.

THE FIRST CIGARETTE: INITIATION

> If a person smokes one cigarette there is about a 70 per cent chance that they will go on to be a smoker. More than one increases that chance to 80 per cent. By the time a person has, say, four cigarettes, they've got a 90 per cent chance of becoming a regular smoker. So the adolescents who are having one or two a week might go on like that while they are still in school and they haven't got a lot of money, but, inevitably, they become regular smokers. (Dr Michael Russell.)

It is well documented that smoking is a habit acquired in either childhood or adolescence. Very few people take it up after the age of twenty. An inquiry on behalf of the UK Department of Health and Social Security by Alan Marsh and Jil Matheson stated:

> Taking up the habit of smoking cigarettes is predominantly a teenage experience. Taking all the smokers and ex-smokers in our sample together, we find that half recall having started to smoke regularly by the time they had passed their sixteenth birthday, three-quarters were smoking at 18, and 90 per cent had acquired a regular smoking habit when they passed their twenty-first birthday. Only 7 per cent of them took up smoking after the age of 25. (*Smoking Attitudes and Behaviour*, 1983.)

Figures in the USA show a similar pattern. It appears that high school and junior high school students are the most susceptible of all to the lure of cigarettes. Cigarette smoking is seen by them as an 'adult' habit. US surveys show that 60 per cent of adult smokers start by the age of fourteen.

Below *Charles Spencelayh painted* A Crafty Smoke *a century ago. Little was then known about the dangers of smoking, but, as today, most smokers took their first cigarette as a child or teenager.*

Above *Girls tend to start smoking at an earlier age than boys and some people believe that they are more vulnerable to advertising claims and pressures than boys. (See page 45).*

In Australia:

- Three-quarters of adults who smoke began smoking when they were adolescents;
- one out of every three adult smokers started smoking before they were nine years old;
- every year 70,000 teenagers become regular smokers;
- each day, more than 500 schoolchildren smoke their first cigarette.

● Why accept the first cigarette?

In trying to find out why people smoke, it is important to understand why they accepted their first cigarette.

> I accepted my first cigarette when I was fifteen. I can't recall smoking it, but it must have pleased me — it was the first of several hundred thousand. At parties, cigarettes were the perfect prop — they gave you something to fiddle with, they provided a variety of opening gambits, and smoking looked so sexy. When I was working for exams, desperate for oral gratification since I was always half-starving myself, I smoked furtively at home. (Judy Sadgrove, Health Editor, the *Guardian*, 7 June, 1989.)

The main reasons for taking the first cigarette seem to be:

- curiosity
- looking grown-up
- pressure from friends (known as peer pressure)
- availability (for example, having parents who smoke)
- being drunk at the time
- calming nerves and controlling mood
- keeping weight down
- gaining confidence
- showing off
- fun
- looking tough

> Children whose parents tell them not to smoke, or children who believe that their parents would disapprove of them smoking, are less likely to smoke than children who do not receive such messages from their parents. Children are also less likely to smoke if their parents do not smoke.

Children often associate smoking with adulthood:

> The median age of first experimentation with cigarettes was 12 years ... Smokers constituted 32 per cent of the teenage children of mothers who smoked, compared with only 23 per cent of the children of non-smoking mothers ... Smoking was found in only 20 per cent of teenagers whose elder brothers or sisters did *not* smoke, but in 43 per cent of teenagers whose older siblings did. The teenagers interviewed thought, on average, that 72 per cent of adults smoked (when the true figure was little over 40 per cent). This provided a clear indication of the extent to which smoking and adulthood were associated in the children's minds. (Heather Ashton and Rob Stepney, *Smoking: Psychology and Pharmacology*, 1982.)

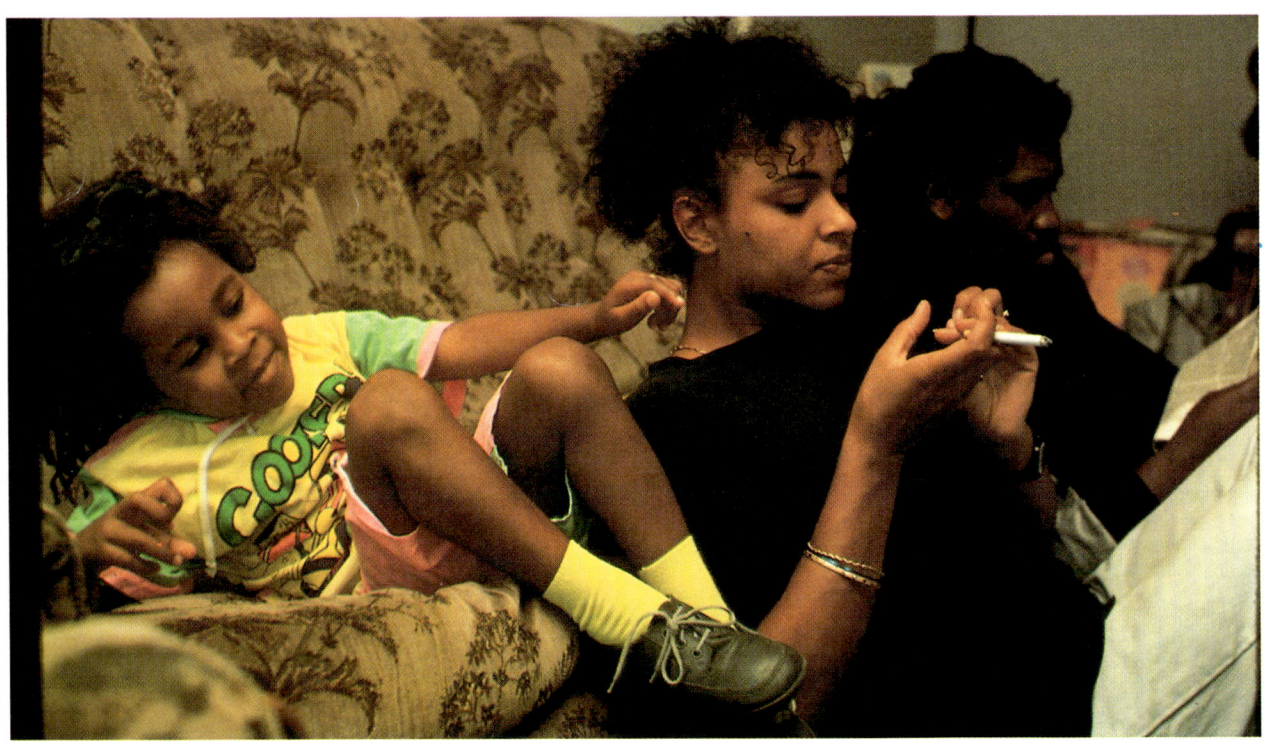

Children may want to smoke in order to seem 'grown up'. Sadly they may well end up having less time to be 'grown up' as smokers, on average, lose 10–15 years of their life.

● 'No man is an island'

A person's behaviour in all aspects of life is influenced by internal factors, such as personality and family attitudes, and by external forces, such as society's rules and pressures. The time between the two world wars was the peak period of cigarette smoking in Europe and the USA. Most people then regarded it as an acceptable habit.

Why people smoke

Right *Audrey Hepburn in the romantic comedy* Breakfast at Tiffany's *(1961) typifies what used to be considered chic and glamorous in earlier decades — swathed in a little black dress and a cloud of smoke.*

> It was only realized in the early fifties that smoking causes cancer and therefore a lot of the people who smoked, and in whom it became an ingrained habit, were fully established smokers before this. A lot of the old boys I see now started smoking during the Second World War, and when they started it was the done thing. It wasn't realized that there were any side-effects to it and in fact it was regarded as being socially a very, very acceptable thing to do. (W J Owen, Consultant Surgeon, Guy's Hospital, London, in an interview with the author, 1989.)

- **The power of advertising**

Television advertising of cigarettes is outlawed in many developed countries, including Australia, Britain and the USA, but advertisers get round this by sponsoring national and international sports events and championships in whichever countries they can. This allows them to display their product on hoardings and racing cars, and even on the clothing of participants, many of whom are international heroes. Being unable to spend money on TV advertising in some countries, tobacco companies have more to spend on space in national newspapers and national magazines.

Some countries no longer permit tobacco advertisements that suggest smoking is sexy and glamorous. To reduce advertisements' appeal to young people, in Britain and in Australia, the people shown in advertisements must be aged over twenty-five, and look over twenty-five. However, in many countries — including the developing world — tobacco promotions frequently associate cigarettes with sex appeal and a glamorous lifestyle.

Sexy images like this one ignore the medical hazards of lung cancer, heart disease, gangrene and ulcers. Does she like him enough to risk her health, perhaps her life? This Australian ad was successful: the company's share of the Australian adolescent market rose from 1 per cent to 27 per cent within a four year period.

Why people smoke

> The advertisements are totally inappropriate because they produce a picture of health. You often get these advertisements showing someone sitting on a horse, beside a lovely cool river, smoking a cigarette. It's a contradiction in attitudes because we all know that smoking is bad for you and yet, in some countries, it's depicted in a sort of situation which produces happiness of mind, body and spirit. So it's a trick, it's a con trick. (W J Owen.)

● **What do the tobacco companies say?**
The tobacco companies claim that:

● advertising does not affect total consumption, but only makes smokers switch brands;
● advertising is aimed only at adults, never at children, and does not encourage non-smokers (either adult or juvenile) to start smoking;
● advertising is necessary to convey 'vital product information' to smokers, such as which brands are low tar, for example.

Tobacco ads often reinforce their message with an appeal to teenage concerns — a young woman's desire to be slim, a young man's to be macho.

Perhaps one of the most famous of smokers: Winston Churchill, UK Prime Minister during the Second World War (1940–45). Churchill is reported to have said that if he had not smoked so much, he would have lost his temper more often. Churchill almost certainly benefited from nicotine's unique capacity to enhance concentration.

> We've found that something like 80 per cent of adolescent smokers said they preferred Benson and Hedges. Their advertisements are quite surreal, you do have to stare at them for a minute or two to work out what on earth they're saying. They are very, very clever adverts. The children's preference of 80 per cent is in marked contrast to that found in adults of 17 per cent. (Dr Ann McNeill, Research Psychologist, Addiction Research Unit, Institute of Psychiatry, London, in an interview with the author, 1989.)

THE ENJOYMENT PHASE

Many people claim to enjoy smoking. However, 90 per cent of smokers have tried to give up smoking at one time or another. The short-term ill effects of smoking (coughing, wheezing, shortness of breath, lack of energy) are not so apparent in the young, so it is usually that group that professes to enjoy the habit.

> Young smokers can offset the short-term bad effects of smoking by training and by taking vigorous exercise. We can measure a child's exposure to tobacco, either through their own smoking or by their exposure to other people's, and they will find the results both surprising and alarming. But it will be a long time before they actually *feel* the damage. (Martin Jarvis, Senior Lecturer and Clinical Psychologist, Imperial Cancer Research Fund, Health Behaviour Unit, Institute of Psychiatry, London, in an interview with the author, 1989.)

Why people smoke

The experts agree that when smokers talk of the 'pleasure' or 'enjoyment' of smoking, they are in fact referring to the relief from the craving for nicotine.

> The exact effect of nicotine is not a thrill, a high, such as amphetamine (speed) or cocaine produces. Nor is it a profoundly calming effect such as heroin. Nicotine has this unique ability to calm and stimulate alternately, according to the circumstances. This, of course, makes it a very versatile drug. It stimulates you when you are bored or tired, and calms you when you are tense. It reduces irritability and improves concentration. To cap it all, smoking a cigarette is a very efficient way of delivering nicotine to the brain. The drug arrives within seven seconds of the first puff. No other drug-delivery method works as quickly. An intravenous injection takes fourteen seconds to get to the brain, and after swallowing a pill there is a delay of twenty to thirty minutes before any mind-altering substance has any effect. (Dr John Cutting, Consultant Psychiatrist, Bethlem Royal and Maudsley Hospitals, in an interview with the author, 1989.)

Is it that the drug is addictive or is the habit more to do with the rituals associated with smoking? In the past, some researchers stressed the psychological aspects of smoking, such as handling the packet, handling the cigarette, having something to do with your hands and putting something in your mouth.

> Handling it and lighting it up and so on are called conditioning factors. These things become satisfying because they are so often *associated with* the satisfaction of the nicotine. The rituals become satisfying in themselves, but if you take away the nicotine they will soon become unsatisfying.
>
> There is a lot of evidence to show that it is the level of nicotine in the blood that is the overriding factor for smoking. Nicotine has psychoactive effects which are potentially rewarding. It alters the level of arousal and alters mood and performance. Thinking and concentration improve. Nicotine is what behavioural scientists call a 'primary reinforcer': that is, humans find it pleasant . . . Sex is a primary reinforcer and so is food. Nicotine acts as a primary reinforcer in that it acts on the reward area of the brain and stimulates that system. If you find something that gives you pleasure, it's natural to continue with it. (Dr Michael Russell.)

Roll-up cigarettes are even more dangerous to health because they usually have no protective filter. Handling rituals were once said to be part of the dependence upon tobacco, but scientific evidence now demonstrates that nicotine alone is responsible for the smoker's addiction.

A real smoker, in contrast to the healthy looking models seen in the ads. It is not long before experimentation with and enjoyment of nicotine turns into addiction. Smoking damages the skin, and stains the fingers and teeth. The repeated sucking action causes lines in the cheeks and around the mouth. All together these effects are known as 'smoker's face'.

ADDICTION

The third stage of development of the smoking habit is addiction. The smoker becomes dependent on nicotine.

> The stage of pure pleasure is short-lived because quite soon — weeks or months at the most — a new state develops. From becoming a casual smoker, able to control mood and attention by the occasional cigarette, the situation is reversed. Rather than the smoker using nicotine to control his/her brain to best advantage, the brain urges the smoker to smoke more and more to feed its appetite for nicotine. This is addiction. The smoker is now a slave of the substance, not its master. (Dr John Cutting.)

> They [teenagers] will probably go on smoking for another thirty or forty years because most people don't give up until they're in their fifties or sixties. Despite the fact that, usually in their middle twenties, they are beginning to become disenchanted with the habit, they go on because they find it difficult to do without it. Then, in their thirties, they often make a serious attempt to stop. So they're trapped after just a few cigarettes. (Dr Michael Russell.)

---

1 What do you think are the main reasons for people starting to smoke?

2 What do you think about the promotion of tobacco products at sports events?

3 What do you think of magazines that devote a lot of space to fashion, health and beauty — and carry advertisements for cigarettes?

4 What would you tell your own children about smoking? At what age do you think you would need to talk to them about it?

3

'I'm dying for a cigarette'

> A custom, lothesome to the eye, hateful to the Nose, harmful to the braine, dangerous to the Lungs and in the black stinking fume thereof, neerest resembling the horrible Stigian smoke of the pit that is bottomelesse . . . by the immoderate taking of tobacco, the wealth of a great number of people is impaired and their bodies unfit for labour. (James I, King of England, 1603.)

Was he right? Joe Califano has referred to the smoking habit as 'slow-motion suicide' and it would be difficult to imagine a doctor anywhere in the world disagreeing with him today.

> We all know that smoking can kill. The statistics show that 100,000 premature deaths each year [in Britain] are caused by smoking. That is 15 to 20 per cent of all deaths in this country. Cigarettes cause lung cancer, chronic bronchitis, emphysema and coronary heart disease, which are all killers. And we know 40 per cent of heavy smokers die before retiring age — this is compared with 15 per cent of non-smokers.
>
> It has been estimated that out of 1,000 young men who smoke in this country [Britain], 1 will be murdered, 6 will die in a road accident and 250 will die prematurely as a result of smoking. The figures are a national disgrace. (Dr John Dawson, Head of British Medical Association's Professional Division.)

The international picture is much the same. So what does the tobacco industry have to say?

> The 'war against cancer' . . . degenerated into a war against cigarettes . . . Now it has further degenerated into a war against smokers, waged through vilification, banishment from public places, denial of employment and repressive taxation. No one really knows whether this . . . warfare against . . . millions . . . will prevent a single case of lung cancer or heart disease . . .
>
> Many people do look for a 'scapegoat' when they feel threatened. In this case it is smoking. We are on the brink of paranoia . . . In the meantime, the quest for knowledge about disease is prejudiced . . . The smoking controversy must be resolved by scientific research. (Tobacco Institute, Washington DC, December, 1978.)

James I (1566–1625) was not a popular king, but he was far-sighted enough to recognize the perils of tobacco nearly 400 years ago.

Perhaps they had not looked at the evidence.

> I just don't believe that anybody could be unconvinced, who's really taken the trouble to look at the evidence. They know they're selling death now. They're not stupid. They just don't choose to admit it. (Sir George Godber, Chief Medical Officer for Health, UK, 1960-72, talking to Peter Taylor, author of *The Smoke Ring: Tobacco, Money and Multinational Politics*, 1985.)

Chief diseases associated with regular smoking

Arteries
- arteriosclerosis (hardening of arteries);
- atherosclerosis (narrowing of arteries due to deposits of fat in their walls);

both of these diseases lead to:

- angina (chest pain on exertion);
- heart attack (severe chest pain and often death);
- gangrene (death of skin and muscle, particularly in limbs, sometimes necessitating amputation);
- stroke (brain damage, causing, in particular, weakness of limbs, loss of speech and confusion).

Lungs
- bronchitis (chronic obstruction of airways to the lungs), causing extreme difficulty in breathing;
- cancer of the lung;
- emphysema (the air sacs of the lungs become grossly enlarged and are eventually destroyed, resulting in difficulty and eventually in inability to breathe).

Digestive System
- cancer of the oesophagus (gullet);
- cancer of the stomach;
- ulcer disease.

Reproductive organs
- cancer of the cervix (neck of the uterus);
- infertility.

Left *The 1962 UK campaign against smoking.*

'I'm dying for a cigarette'

Chief effects of smoking tobacco on a healthy person

Heart and circulation
- rise in blood pressure;
- increase in pulse rate;
- irregular heart beat;
- reduced efficiency of red blood cells responsible for carrying oxygen around the body: 15 per cent of them are subverted into carrying the carbon monoxide produced by smoke.

Digestive (gastrointestinal) system
- decreased appetite;
- constipation.

Brain and spinal cord (central nervous system)
- stimulation or depression of nervous system, depending on mood.

A study by Richard Doll and Professor A Bradford Hill in Britain in 1952 was a landmark in the scientific enquiry into the effects of smoking. They assessed 5,000 hospital patients; of the 1,357 who had cancer of the lung, only 7 were non-smokers.

> Amongst men of ages 45 to 64 the death-rate in non-smokers is negligible, while in the heavier-smoking categories it is estimated to reach 3 to 5 deaths per annum per 1,000 living . . . it is concluded that the association between smoking and carcinoma of the lung is real. (Doll and Hill, *British Medical Journal*, 13 December, 1952.)

In 1964, a report by the advisory committee to US Surgeon General Dr Luther Terry concluded:

> Cigarette smoking is causally related to lung cancer in men . . . [It] is the most important of the causes of chronic bronchitis in the United States, and increases the risk of dying from chronic bronchitis and emphysema. (*Smoking and Health*, Report of the Advisory Committee to the US Surgeon General, US Public Health Service, 1964.)

● What is in tobacco smoke?

> *Cancer-causing agents* (carcinogens): there are dozens of carcinogens in tobacco smoke. One of the most potent of all carcinogens is benzopyrene, discovered in tobacco smoke over thirty years ago.
>
> *Carbon monoxide*: this is a poisonous gas which lowers the amount of oxygen carried by the blood. It does this by occupying the positions on red blood cells that are normally occupied by oxygen when it is carried around in the blood.
>
> *Nicotine*: this is the addictive drug which maintains the tobacco habit. It makes the heart beat faster and work harder than it should, and it adversely affects blood-clotting factors which may play a part in heart attacks.
>
> *Radioactive compounds*: the radioactive compounds found in highest concentration in cigarette smoke are polonium 210 and potassium 40. Radioactive compounds are well known to cause cancer.
>
> *Hydrogen cyanide*: this is the gas used as a means of execution in American gas chambers. In the amounts found in tobacco smoke, it kills cilia, the tiny hairs that move together in waves to help keep our lungs clean.

Below *Nicotine causes the addiction, but tar causes cancer.*

Pesticides: a range of pesticides have been found in tobacco, including DDT, endrin, parathion and endosulfan.

Metals: many toxic metals, including arsenic and nickel, have been found in cigarette smoke. (National Heart Foundation of Australia.)

- **What does smoking do to your body?**

The dangers of smoking have been known for some time:

> When tobacco is burnt or smoked, the tar is vaporized so that it becomes very, very small particles. These are inhaled along with lots of other chemicals. When the smoke cools, the tar condenses and becomes recognizable tar again. The unfortunate thing about tar is that it's carcinogenic ... Cancer of the lung is a very, very rare illness in non-smokers ... it's almost entirely due to cigarette smoking. (Michael Belcher, Clinical Nurse Specialist, Smokers' Clinic, the Maudsley Hospital, London, in an interview with the author, 1989.)

In Australia in 1986, the following body organs were removed from humans because of cancer caused by smoking:

521 lungs
148 gullets
 71 tongues
221 voice boxes
 82 stomachs
 40 pancreases
 68 wombs
 85 bladders
115 kidneys
161 miscellaneous body parts

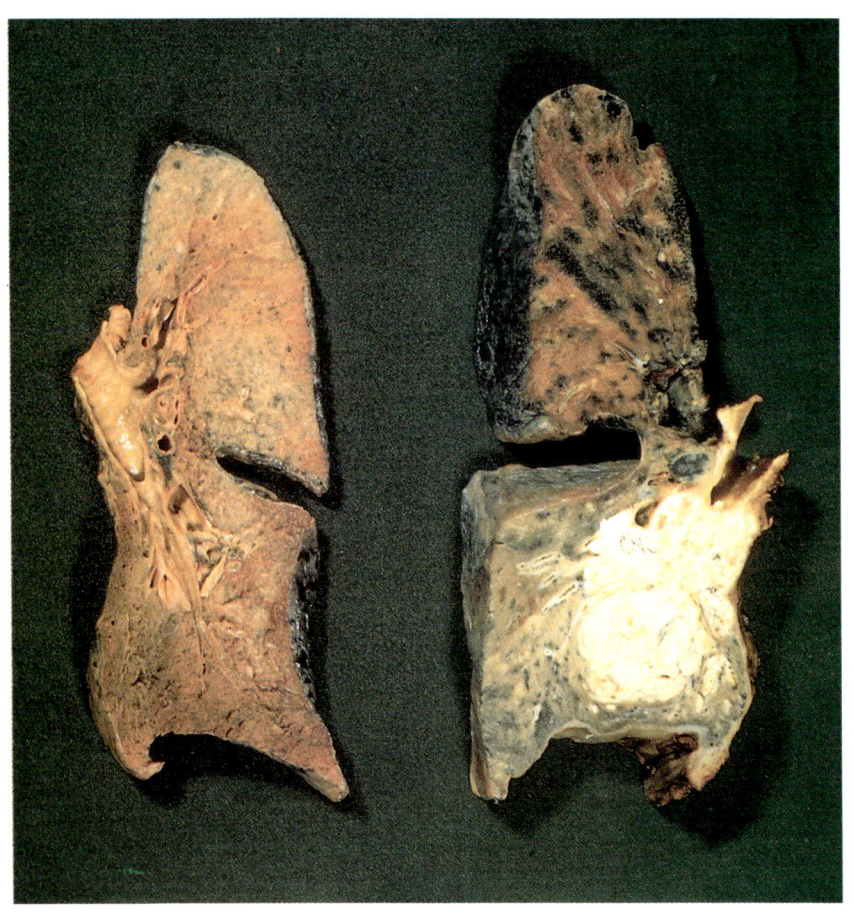

A normal lung (left) at postmortem and a lung destroyed by cancer (right). The tumour, or cancerous growth, appears as a white mass in the lower lobe (part) of the cancerous lung. The tissue in the upper lobe is blackened by tar deposits from cigarette smoking. The more cigarettes a smoker smokes, the more likely it is that lung cancer will develop.

'I'm dying for a cigarette'

Tar, together with other substances taken in by smokers, damages the tiny hairs in the lungs called cilia. These hairs keep the lungs clean, sweeping germs and dirt up and out of them. Once the hairs are tarred up, they can no longer do this. This is why smokers are especially prone to chest infections.

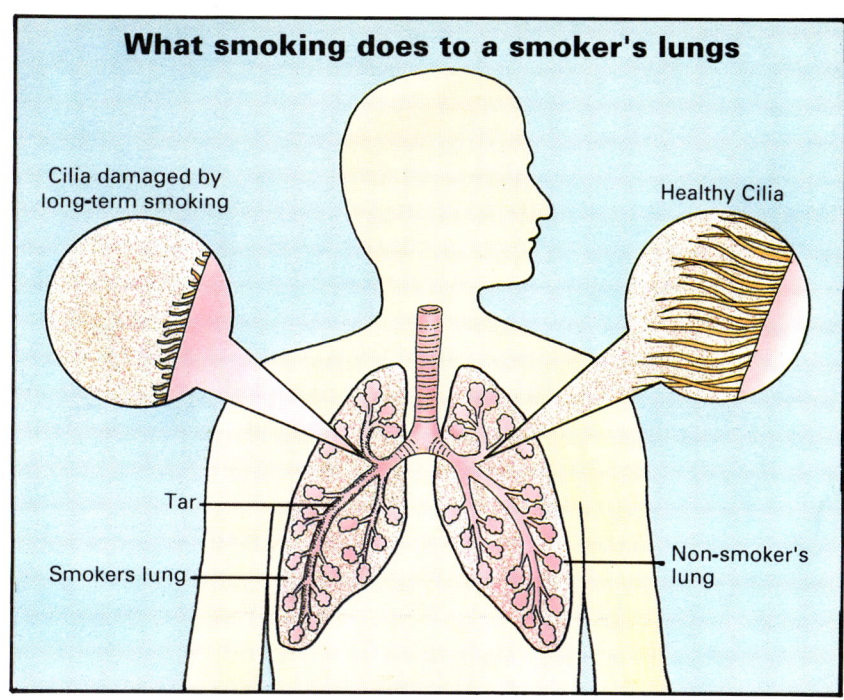

Smoking-related disease loses 50 million working days per year in the UK.

The British National Health Service cost £26 billion for the year 1989-90; of this £500 million was to treat smoking-related disease.

Smoking causes a number of other diseases:

> Cigarette smoking is causally related to lung cancer in both men and women . . . is a significant causative factor in cancer of the larynx . . . is a significant causal factor in the development of oral cancer . . . is a causal factor in the development of cancer of the oesophagus . . . is related to cancer of the pancreas . . . is one of the three major independent risk factors for heart attack . . . and sudden cardiac death in adult men and women . . . a cause of chronic obstructive lung disease . . . increases the risk of fetal death through maternal complications . . . contributes to the risk of their infants being victims of the 'sudden infant death syndrome' [cot death]. (*Smoking and Health*, Report of the US Surgeon General, 1979.)

> Smoking is certainly the major cause of bronchitis and cancer. Ninety-five per cent of patients with blocked arteries to the legs are smokers . . . If the arteries become completely blocked, the foot (or toe) turns black — gangrenous — and has to be amputated. The same problem happens to the arteries supplying the heart and the brain . . . If the artery becomes entirely blocked, the area of heart muscle which it was feeding dies off and this is what a heart attack is. The patient may then die, either because this disturbs the heart beat mechanism or

Ninety-five per cent of cases of gangrene occur in smokers. A smoker's arteries can become harder and narrower, and so eventually become blocked. When that happens to the arteries supplying the limbs, the fingers or toes turn black, and must be amputated.

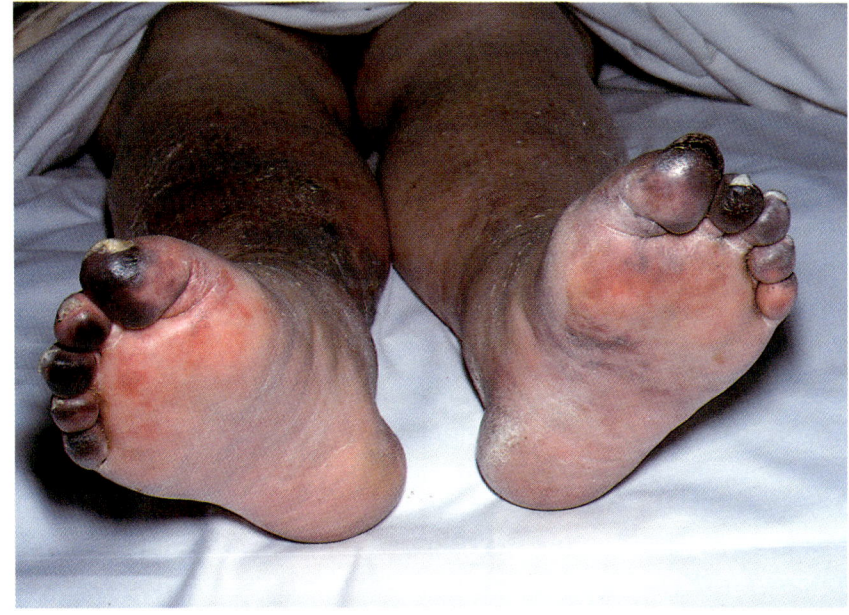

because the amount of heart muscle killed off is so great that the heart can't pump properly – heart failure. If the arteries to the brain narrow or become blocked, the part of the brain which was being supplied dies and this is known as a stroke. Some of the less well-known diseases caused by smoking include cancer of the oesophagus, inflammation of the oesophagus and peptic ulcer disease. (W J Owen.)

One in five men and one in ten women suffer from ulcers at some time in their life:

> . . . smokers are twice as likely as non-smokers to develop ulcers, they respond less well to treatment and they are more likely to develop complications. (Anne Charlish and Dr Brian Gazzard, Consultant Physician, St Stephen's and Westminster Hospitals, London, *How to Cure Your Ulcer*, 1988.)

- **'I don't believe it is bad for you'**
> I know a chap of eighty-two who's smoked all his life and he's in the best of health . . .
> My mum smokes two packs a day and she's fine, she has a busy job and she always looks good . . .
> We've all got to die sometime . . .

All of us have heard these sorts of statements many times over.

> One might as well say that, because several thousand people survived Auschwitz, it wasn't harmful to the three million

---

1 Do you think the health warnings on cigarette packets and advertisements for tobacco products tell you enough about the risks to your health?

2 How would you feel if one of your brothers or sisters, or other young close relatives, started smoking?

3 Ask some of the smokers you know to list the health hazards of smoking and compare their answers with what you now know.

4 Why do you think that 40 per cent of smokers, compared with 15 per cent of non-smokers, die before the age of 65?

'I'm dying for a cigarette'

people who died there. There are always a lucky few who survive a disaster. You may survive walking across a six-lane motorway, but no one in their right mind would do it. (Dr John Cutting.)

Some people believe that just because they are not suffering any current ill effects they never will:

> Well, I suppose I smoke thirty a day or so and I don't feel any bad effects . . . but they're always telling you something's bad for you, aren't they? I enjoy my job, I play tennis in the summer and I ride and swim all year round. (Liz, aged twenty-four.)

> Young people can to some extent offset their decreased oxygen levels by vigorous exercise. Vigorous exercise makes the heart work harder, producing freshly oxygenated blood . . . The good news is that most of the effects on their respiratory systems will be reversible. The younger they give up, the more reversal there will be, but not all effects on lung function are reversible. There is now some evidence that the heart-disease risk persists for quite a long time after you give up, so that you carry your history as a smoker with you for quite a few years after. The damage that's been done to your arteries doesn't just all go away. (Martin Jarvis.)

A smoker of ten cigarettes a day is much more likely to die from a smoking-related disease than from any kind of violence or any accident.

Comparing causes of death in the USA

AIDS 8,959
Homicides 21,400
Suicides 31,470
Motor vehicle deaths 48,560
Tobacco-related deaths 350,000

SOURCE: US Centers for Disease Control, 1986 figures

These figures show that in 1986 by far the most dangerous activity in the USA was smoking.

Why do people take such risks?

> Some things *seem* much riskier than others. Many people are scared of going on aeroplanes, but it's not a very risky thing to do, it's actually much riskier to drive to your local shopping centre . . . but it doesn't *feel* that way. One of the problems about smoking is that it doesn't *feel* very risky, although it's actually about the riskiest thing you can do. (Martin Jarvis.)

'It's my life, isn't it?'

> Look, if I want to kill myself smoking, that's my problem, isn't it? (Dave, aged thirty-four.)

Many smokers argue that it is up to them if they choose to damage their health, but smoking in public, particularly in confined spaces, is a problem for non-smokers and ex-smokers as well. They suffer the harmful effects of other people's tobacco smoke through forced smoking. Forced smokers do not smoke voluntarily: they smoke passively. In other words, they inhale tobacco smoke and damage their health involuntarily. Many non-smokers object to this, maintaining that a smoker has no right to damage other people's health. Smokers, on the other hand, defend their right to smoke.

Should an individual always have the right to personal freedom or should society curtail that freedom when it leads to behaviour that is harmful to others?

Where smokers and non-smokers work together, the non-smokers run serious health risks through passive smoking, and besides they finish the day with their hair and clothes reeking of other people's smoke.

'It's my life, isn't it?'

Now that the risks of passive smoking are known, is it fair for a smoker to claim, 'It's my life, isn't it?'

● The risks of passive smoking

A British study published in 1989, 'Smoking among secondary school children in 1988', reported that those children whose parents both smoke have a nicotine level equivalent to smoking two cigarettes each week, even though they themselves do not smoke.

> Non-smokers who are exposed to other people's smoke have about a 30 per cent increase in their risk of getting lung cancer. That means there are something like 300 or so lung cancer deaths in non-smokers in the UK every year due to passive smoking, and maybe up to 1,000 deaths altogether per year from passive smoking. We get extremely agitated about maybe 20 leukaemia deaths associated with the nuclear industry over a period of 20 years — and this is of course of immense public concern — yet over that period we are talking about nearly 20,000 deaths from passive smoking. But somehow they're kind of invisible. (Martin Jarvis.)

Another large study, published in 1989 by the *British Medical Journal*, confirms the hazard of passive smoking. The Cancer Surveillance Unit at Ruchill Hospital, Glasgow, found that living with someone who smokes doubles the risk of heart disease, adversely affects the heart, circulation and breathing and substantially increases the non-smoker's chances of developing lung cancer.

> I've suffered with asthma for many, many years, so I have to avoid smoky atmospheres. The smoke irritates the airways, you see, and causes spasm which brings on an attack. It's very frightening . . . I can't get my breath at all. (Dorothy, aged seventy-three.)

Passive smokers run many of the health risks that smokers do (see chapter 3) and many of them also suffer sore or runny eyes, sneezing, runny nose, blocked-up nose, headache, coughing, wheezing, hoarseness and allergy. The children of smokers are more likely than the children of non-smokers to develop bronchitis, pneumonia and other chest infections.

Is it fair to non-smokers to inflict all these risks on them? And is it fair to ex-smokers? Having fought addiction, inhaling other people's tobacco smoke might tempt them to restart the habit.

Passive smoking causes skin diseases, such as allergic dermatitis, in smokers' dogs. Both dogs and cats can develop respiratory infections through passive smoking.

No one is 'forced' to go to a restaurant—so some restaurant owners say that if people do not like smoke they do not have to go to their restaurant. Others feel that smoking in restaurants is unpleasant, unhealthy and ruins the taste of the food—and so should be stopped.

● Personal freedom

Should smokers be forced to curtail their smoking?

> I've never cared much for fashionable causes . . . I don't smoke . . . but I do care about personal freedom . . . and what a fundamental right it is to choose to smoke. (Stephen Eyres, Director of the Freedom Association for the Right to Enjoy Smoking Tobacco [FOREST], in FOREST Newsletter No.5, January 1982.)

> Those who continue to smoke have decided that the pleasure they experience is worth the risks and such is their democratic right. (Timothy Evans in *The Right to Smoke*, published by FOREST.)

Why does FOREST feel the need to defend a smoker's personal freedom?

> FOREST is an organization sponsored by the tobacco industry. The freedoms they are concerned with are the freedoms of the tobacco manufacturers to go on pushing their lethal products. (David Simpson, Director of Action on Smoking and Health [ASH], in an interview with the author, 1989.)

However, there are many people, including some non-smokers and ex-smokers, who believe that people should be free to smoke.

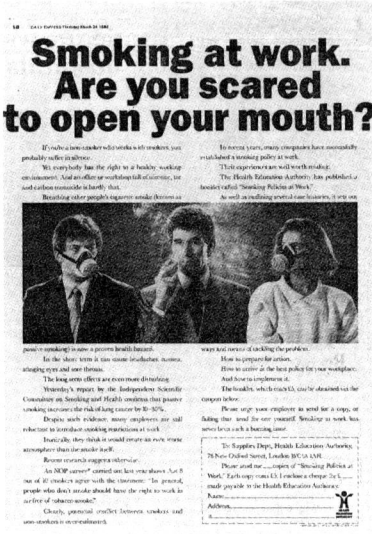

Above *The Health Education Authority's response to the TAC's argument (**below**, **left**). This full page advertisement in a newspaper points out, among other things, that in a national survey, 8 out of 10 smokers felt that non-smokers have the right to work in air free of tobacco smoke.*

Left *An advertisement placed in national newspapers by the Tobacco Advisory Council (TAC). The TAC's function is to promote tobacco. The statement shown here is contradicted by scientific evidence which shows passive smoking as a cause of lung cancer (see previous page).*

Right *This pregnant woman is making her unborn child smoke. The poisonous substances are entering the child's bloodstream. She is running the risk of miscarriage or a stillbirth. (See below.)*

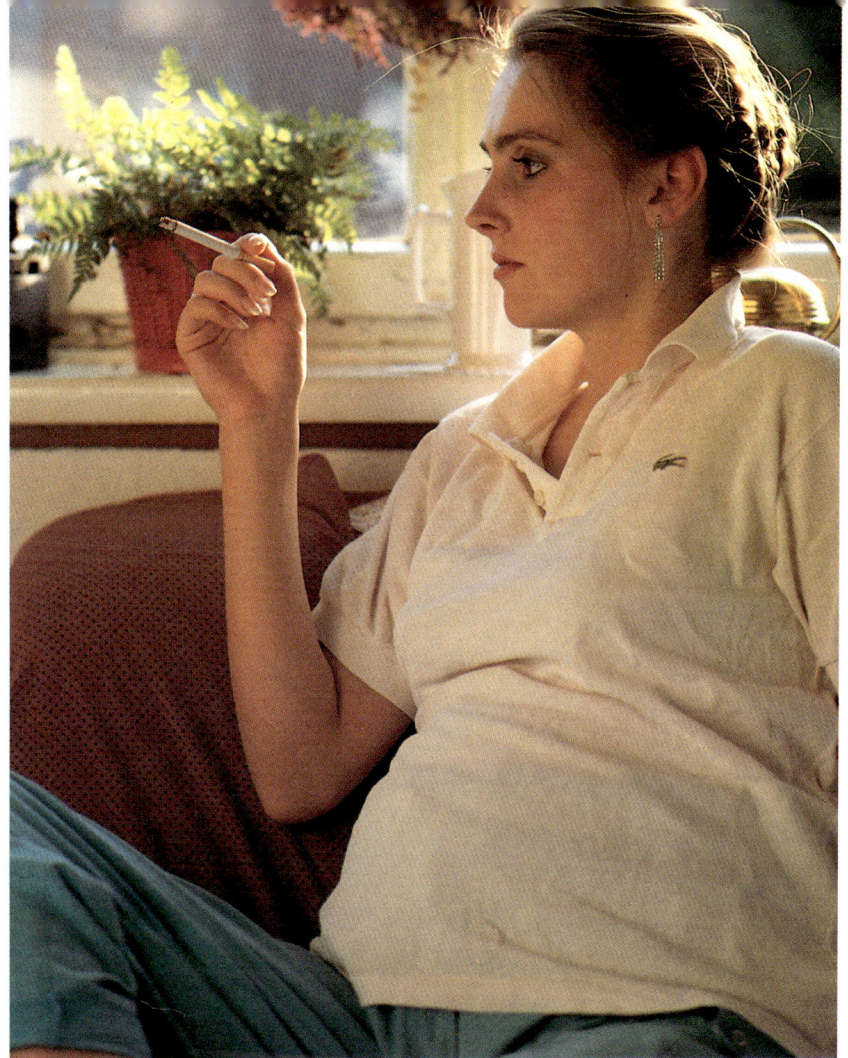

- **No chance to choose**

However, this freedom can exist only if others sacrifice their right to a smoke-free environment. In some cases they have no choice:

> What would you think if we made a new-born baby smoke a cigarette? You know everyone would be horrified, yet when a pregnant woman smokes that's exactly what she is doing. A lot of the smoke toxins are carried directly to the fetus. (Martin Jarvis.)

> If a woman who is expecting a baby smokes, the nicotine and carbon monoxide from each cigarette pass into the bloodstream and thus into the fetus. The nicotine makes the baby's heart beat faster. The carbon monoxide causes less oxygen to get to the baby. So, if women continue to smoke throughout pregnancy, there is an increased risk of miscarriage, low birth weight and neonatal mortality [death of the baby soon after birth]. (Scottish Health Education Group.)

> The evidence of increased risk of pneumonia and bronchitis in infants with smoking mothers is now unequivocal, but there are also other health problems in the first year of life which have been shown to be increased by parental smoking. Impaired lung function, increased incidence of coughs and general respiratory disorders have also been shown in smokers' children. (Dr Anne Charlton, Director of Cancer Research Campaign Education and Child Studies Research Group, University of Manchester, England, in an interview with the author, 1989.)

Finally, the chances of cot death (known as sudden infant death syndrome) double if the mother smokes during pregnancy.

Just in case the message had not got through, some health warnings on cigarette packets spell out the dangers of smoking while pregnant. Doctors now advise women to give up smoking before trying to conceive.

Many children in developed countries are already aware of the dangers of smoking and are frightened for their parents' health. Some know that the biggest single cause of death in their fathers' age-group (middle-aged men) is smoking.

> Both of my parents smoke, and for years I have done my best to dissuade them from their addiction. I have pointed out the dangers, shown them facts, and admittedly they are cutting down. But they can't turn back the clock to that first cigarette and say 'no'. Just like they won't be able to turn back the clock when they are dying of lung cancer or some other deadly disease. (Holly Allen, aged fourteen, in her project on smoking, at Notre Dame School, Lingfield, Surrey, 1989.)

This woman already knows of the dangers to her baby's health if she — or others — smoke near it. So she's supporting the Great American Smokeout, a day when people across the country are asked not to smoke.

A doctor points out the risks for children whose mother smokes heavily:

> She's making them [her four children] smoke passively, so they're in for chest trouble, but the big thing will be if she gets lung cancer or an early heart attack. What are those smashing kids going to do without her? She's not a monster, she's a lovely mum, but she just says 'I smoked since I was fourteen and I can't give it up.' (Dr Frances Parrish, general practitioner, Sussex, England, in an interview with the author, 1989.)

Do smokers hold some responsibility for the health of future generations? Seeing adults smoking can give children the impression that it is safe, acceptable and 'grown-up'.

● Clearing the air

In most countries about one-third of the adult population smokes. Two-thirds do not. Many people would welcome a smoke-free environment, particularly in places of work and study, in public places such as shops, restaurants and places of entertainment, and in all forms of public transport.

Several huge problems face those trying to create such an environment. The easy availability and relatively low cost of tobacco products are two crucial factors in determining who tries smoking and who continues. While cigarettes remain comparatively cheap and easily available, it is difficult to convince people of the health risks and to persuade them that smoking is socially unacceptable.

In the UK, surveys show that in some areas eight out of ten tobacconists will sell cigarettes to children under sixteen, even though it is illegal to do so.

> One of the things we were interested in was whether children can buy cigarettes from shops, which of course is illegal. It came out in our survey that a lot of them bought single cigarettes. It appears that tobacconists are actually opening packets and selling cigarettes at 10p or 12p [when a pack of twenty costs about £1.50] and making an incredible profit and, therefore, are actively pushing them. (Dr Ann McNeill.)
> One big, big mistake is not to put the price up. That's really important in stopping children smoking and stopping rising consumption. (Dr Chris Steele.)

Children and parents at the UK launch of the pressure group Parents Against Tobacco (PAT) in 1990. PAT wants new laws to make it extremely difficult for the tobacco industry's ads and promotions to reach children. PAT is also campaigning for stricter enforcement of the laws against the sale of cigarettes to children. It is estimated that in the UK, children spend £70 million per year on cigarettes.

A further problem for those trying to create a smoke-free environment is that tobacco products are openly advertised and promoted. This too can give children the impression that smoking is both safe and acceptable. If it is not, they ask, why are cigarettes advertised and why are they on sale? Why, in other words, do they seem to be an accepted part of our environment? One of the specific problems in this context is the sponsorship of sporting events by tobacco companies. In return for their sponsorship, the companies get the name of their products emblazoned on the race-track, racing car, backdrop, clothing and, indeed, any usable surface. Why do they advertise in this way?

'It's my life, isn't it?'

Above *Although tobacco ads on television are banned in some countries, companies get around this by sponsoring those sports events that they know will be televised. Here we see a formula one racing car sponsored by a French cigarette company.*

Government revenue from tobacco in the UK is over £5 billion per year. The tobacco industry spends £100 million per year on advertising and promotion in the UK.

> Advertising aims, in the most direct and cost-beneficial way, to change consumer preference. What our critics tend to ignore is that investment in sport is neither a direct nor a cost-beneficial method of influencing consumer preference, and we would be foolish to imagine it was.
>
> Motor racing brings thrills and pleasure to millions of people worldwide. It is also the only appropriate vehicle for simultaneous international communication with our consumers, whatever their language and politics. (Aleardo Buzzi, EEC President of Philip Morris, manufacturer of Marlboro cigarettes, reported in *Autosport*, 28 May, 1987.)

But:

> The tobacco industry says it does not want children to smoke; it also, through the Tobacco Advisory Council, points out that sport depends heavily on sponsorship and, by implication, sport would be poorer if sponsorship was withdrawn. If there is any risk of these two aspects conflicting, the truly altruistic move for the industry would surely be to sponsor sports tacitly, without visible advertising. Does the tobacco industry care enough about sport and children to do this? (Dr Anne Charlton.)

Many people now support the concept of a smoke-free environment and realize that the air we breathe could be healthier than it is.

> Opinion polls [in Britain] now show that at least 75 per cent of the public agree that smoking is a health hazard for everyone; 81 per cent of smokers (and 86 per cent of non-smokers) think non-smokers have the right to work in smoke-free air; 66 per cent believe there should be no smoking on public transport and 91 per cent think all restaurants should provide no-smoking areas . . . but there's a long way to go yet. (David Simpson, ASH.)

The USA has stood up for its non-smokers. Clean Air Acts, restricting smoking in enclosed public places, have been introduced by some states. More than half of USA companies have restricted smoking at work, and some have banned it altogether. There are even companies that refuse to employ smokers.

Will British employers follow suit?

> Over a hundred employers a month are coming to us [ASH] for help with implementing a non-smoking policy. Three years ago there were not many employers, and only twenty to thirty employees a month, coming to us with complaints. Now all this will result in the British work place becoming increasingly non-smoking. I have no doubt at all that in just a few years from now, early in the 1990s, that it will be the rule that you can't smoke at work. (David Simpson, ASH.)

● **Conflicting priorities?**

Not everyone wants a smoke-free environment. Obviously tobacco companies do not. They encourage people to smoke, spending £100 million a year in the UK alone on tobacco advertisements and promotions. Some governments also gain from smoking. While they may issue warnings stating that smoking is harmful, many of them receive revenue through tax on tobacco products.

Let's look at the British example.

> Our government makes £15.5 million a *day* from tobacco tax. They charge 74 per cent tax on every packet sold. Smoking costs the health service £1.5 million a day, so the government ends up with a profit of £14 million a day. Of course they [the government] can't afford to give it up. (Dr Chris Steele.)

Below *Profit to the industry. Profit to the shop selling the product. Profit to the government through taxes. This ad was placed in an Australian trade magazine distributed to cigarette shops.*

'It's my life, isn't it?'

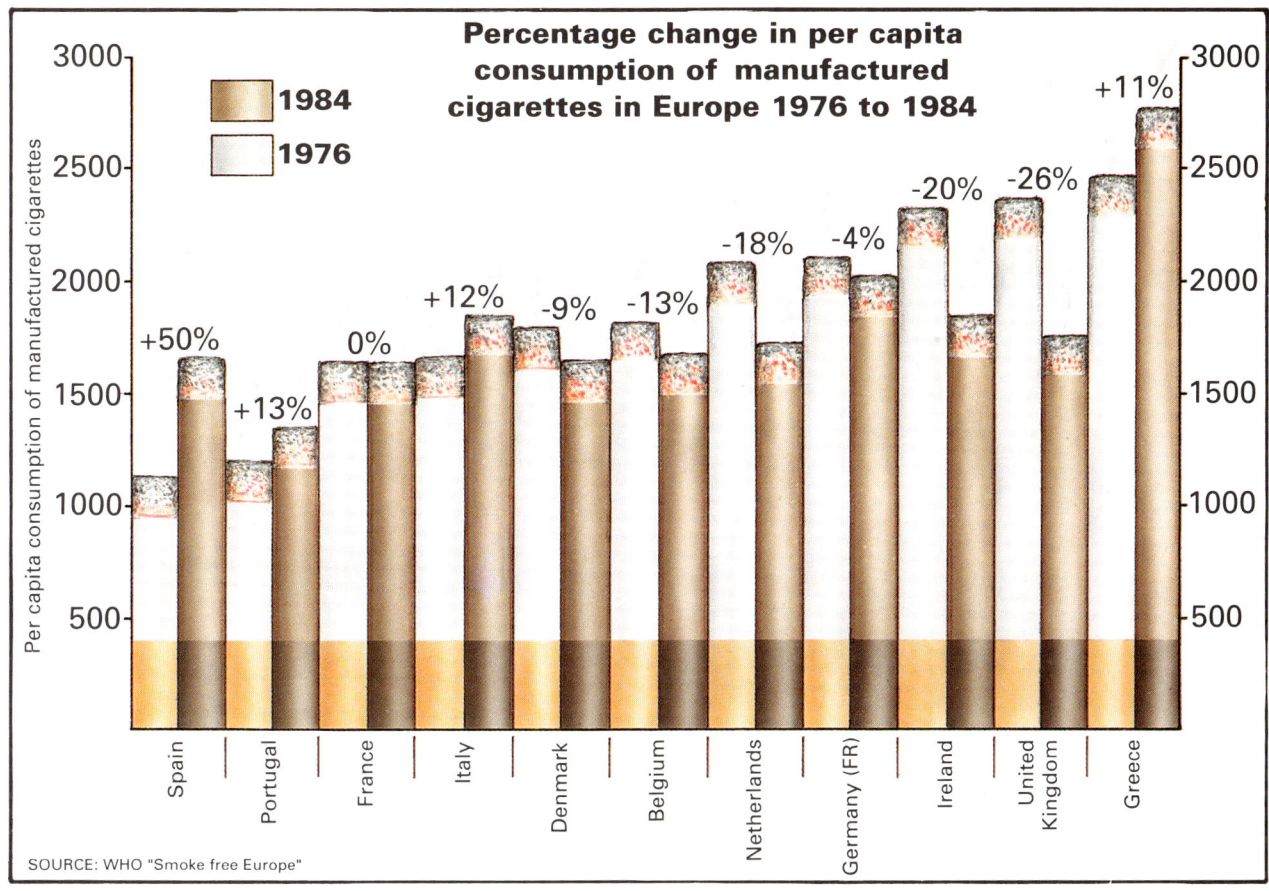

In 1989 the UK Secretary of State for Health, Kenneth Clarke, resisted the introduction of a compulsory 'smoking kills' warning on cigarette packets. At the time, he was rebuked for smoking in public by the chairman of the British Medical Association Council. Clarke's reply:

> I do not at the moment feel inclined to give up smoking because I find the habit relaxing, in the most childish way, in the course of busy days. (Reported in the *Guardian*, 8 March, 1989.)

Like many people in the public eye, Kenneth Clarke has an obvious and important reason to give up smoking, but it seems he cannot do so. If a Minister of Health smokes in public, how can anyone hope to influence young people not to smoke?

In contrast to Kenneth Clarke, Dr Everett Koop, in his capacity as US Surgeon General, was an active champion of the non-smoker's rights. In his years of office (1982-9), Koop saw the number of anti-smoking regulations in the USA rise to 380, with no-smoking areas designated in many public places and places of work.

The level of cigarette consumption can vary dramatically from country to country. Consumption tends to follow price — that is, if the price goes up people smoke less. In the UK, heavy taxes and anti-smoking education combined to produce the largest fall in cigarette consumption in this survey of European countries.

> The evidence ... on the links between passive smoking and lung cancer in non-smokers suggests that 3,800 lung cancer deaths [a year] are caused by passive smoking ... in the US.
>
> Such evidence has provided a weapon to administrators. Ten of the US states are now 'clean-air' states, where you may only smoke in certain public places. Dr Koop's aim was to make the whole of the US a 'clean-air' zone by 2000.
>
> Ask Dr Koop what has driven him in his campaign against smoking and he answers: 'The absolute sleaze of the tobacco companies'. (Aileen Ballantyne, the *Guardian*, 17 July, 1989.)

Dr Koop has not been asked to serve another term as US Surgeon General. Many believe it is because he has been too outspoken about the tobacco business and the dangers of smoking.

The American Nonsmokers' Rights Foundation (ANR) fights on, however, much as Billboard Utilizing Graffitists Against Unhealthy Promotions (BUGA UP) does in Australia. ANR has developed an educational programme, 'Teens as Teachers', enlisting high-school students to teach younger children smoking prevention. BUGA UP 'improves' tobacco advertising messages with 'invention, wit and a spray can', sometimes beyond the limit of the law. Dr Arthur Chesterfield-Evans, President of the Non-Smokers Movement of Australia, was convicted of defacing a tobacco poster and fined $20. The judge told him at the time, 'A person with your integrity can take the verdict as an honour.' The doctor continues his campaign and is now the star of a health promotion video for schools, *Confessions of a Simple Surgeon*.

Below *An example of the work of BUGA UP, on a billboard in Australia.*

'It's my life, isn't it?'

● Are tobacco companies liable?

If governments cannot or will not protect us from the promotion and sale of lethal products, the individual is left to take action, by suing either a tobacco company under product liability laws or an employer under employment laws.

In Britain, non-smokers constantly exposed to smoking colleagues can now take an employer to court. In Sweden a case in 1987 led to lung cancer, in a non-smoker due to passive smoking in the work place, being classified as an occupational injury.

> MELBOURNE [Australia]: An out-of-court settlement awarding a Melbourne bus driver [Sean Carroll] $65,000 because he contracted lung cancer from his passengers' cigarettes could shock employers into banning smoking at work. (The *Sydney Morning Herald*, 22 July, 1988.)

But what about the liability of the tobacco companies?

> A federal jury in Newark, New Jersey, awarded US$400,000 in damages on Monday to Antonio Cipollone, whose wife, Rose, died of lung cancer in 1984 at age fifty-eight. She had smoked a pack and a half of cigarettes a day for forty years. (Reported in *International Herald Tribune*, 15 June, 1988.)

This was the first time a tobacco company was found liable for a smoker's death, but the question of liability is far from settled. In January 1990 the above verdict was overturned. It remains to be seen whether tobacco companies will be held liable, in the USA or elsewhere.

---

1 Do you think smokers should have the right to enjoy smoking tobacco where they work and in public places?

2 Do you believe that investment in sport by tobacco companies is 'neither direct nor cost beneficial'? Why do you think they do it?

3 Why do you think tobacco products are legal but other drugs, such as heroin, are illegal?

4 'Why doesn't the Chancellor [the UK finance minister], put an extra 5p on a packet of cigarettes, thereby providing extra revenue of £200 million – enough to pay for all the sports and arts events currently sponsored by the tobacco companies and all the national health educational programmes and smoking research as well?' (David Simpson, Director of ASH.) Discuss.

5 Why do you think all governments express profound horror at deaths caused by terrorism and natural disasters, but not at the very much larger number of deaths caused by smoking?

This quaint sign from an American cinema is already looking outdated: in many cinemas these days, the rule is no smoking – on both sides of the house!

Giving up

> Not nearly enough is done to help smokers. Many people simply don't understand the problems. Your brain registers almost instant pleasure as you take your first puff of the day. (Dr Chris Steele.)

Discouraging smoking involves:
- continuing the campaign for a smoke-free environment;
- encouraging politicians to press for more strongly worded health warnings on tobacco products, and a ban on all tobacco advertisements and promotion;
- halting investment in the tobacco industry by refusing to purchase their products or invest in their companies;
- persuading employers to look at stop-smoking programmes and to instigate the gradual introduction of designated non-smoking areas, followed eventually by smoke-free work places with designated areas for smokers;
- sympathetically encouraging individual smokers to give up, for their own health and for that of their families, friends and colleagues.

Between 1975 and 1985 the number of American high-school seniors who smoked dropped from 29 per cent to 19.5 per cent.

For those trying to give up, there can be times when the urge to smoke can be very powerful — especially when under pressure, such as during exams. Giving up should be planned for a time free from especially stressful events.

One way to encourage people to give up is to convince them of the drawbacks. This poster from the American Cancer Society flies in the face of the attractive image advertisers associate with smoking.

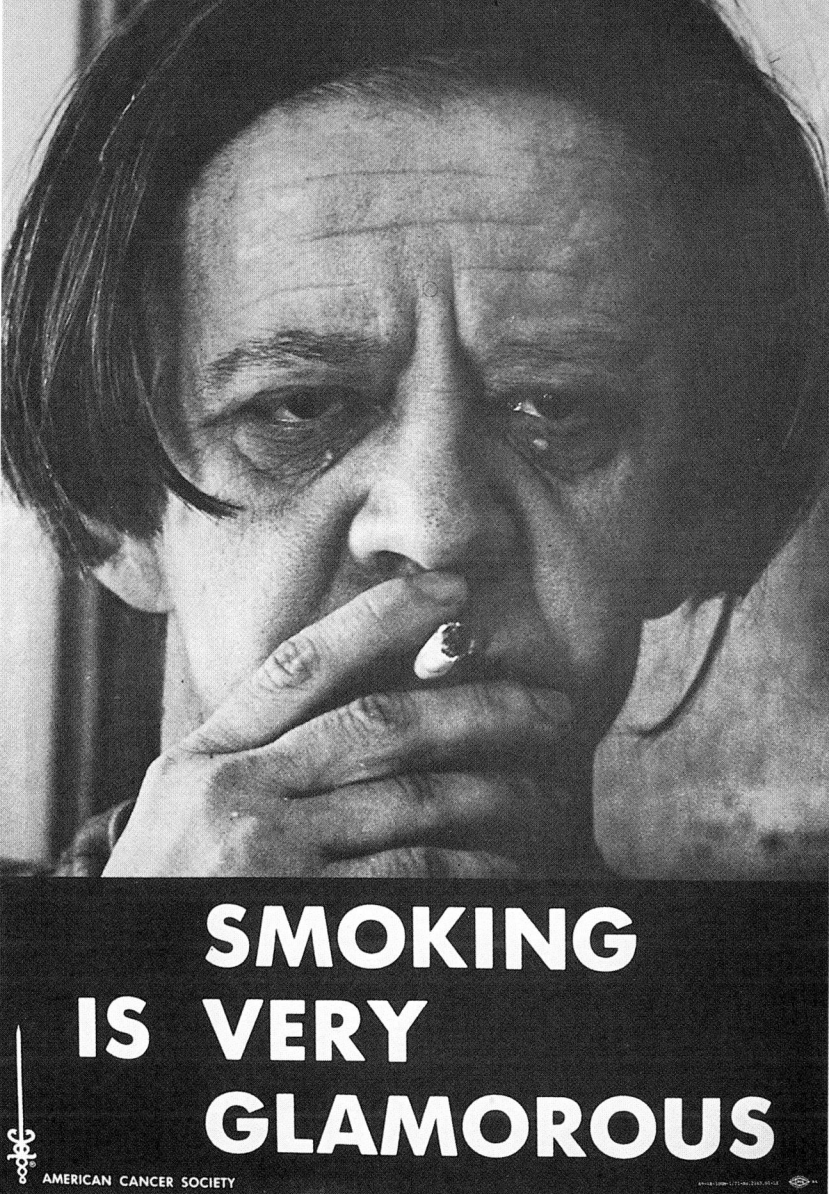

- **Is it difficult to give up smoking?**
> Oh well, it's all in the mind, isn't it? I used to smoke, you know, and I gave it up just like that. (Shirley, aged fifty-two.)

And what do doctors say?
> Well, as I don't smoke, I don't realize how difficult it is to give up, except from talking to people and trying to persuade people, who are otherwise very sensible and reasonable people, to give up when they are clearly aware of the damage it has caused them . . . I'm talking about some of the amputation cases I see. They can see the effect of it but, despite those very strong messages, they are unable to give up; . . . it just points to the addictive nature of the condition.

Doctors were the first group of people to stop smoking. In the UK the number of doctors who smoke has dropped from over 60 per cent to 18 per cent in the last twenty years.

> At least 75 per cent of smokers would like to stop. Smokers who start smoking when young are less likely to give up than those who begin when older.
>
> 25 per cent of smokers say they do not believe smoking is harmful.

After 1952 when cancer was first linked to smoking the first group of people who stopped smoking were doctors. But even now you see some doctors who are involved in looking after smoking-related disease cases who themselves smoke heavily and cannot give up. So you've really got to appreciate, I think, how difficult it is to give up. (W J Owen.)

> Only a third of regular smokers will give up before the age of sixty. One always hears about how many millions of smokers have given up, but most of those who have given up are elderly. (Dr Michael Russell.)

Motivation is a crucial factor in conquering smoking: smokers have to want to give up more than anything else and then to give that goal their undivided attention.

> People don't give up permanently at a young age and I think it's purely because their motivation is low: (a) the health risks are remote; (b) they're hooked already; (c) their priorities are constantly changing. It's much more important to them that they get on well with their current lover or whether they're getting self-respect in their relevant peer groups. That's much more important to them than whether they live to be seventy instead of sixty . . . once teenage smokers are hooked, it's not that they can't stop; you can overcome an addiction, but it does require an effort and a persistent effort which requires not only good motivation, but persistent motivation. (Dr Michael Russell.)

● How to give up

Firstly, it is important to identify the reasons why someone smokes, where they smoke and when they are most at risk, so that they can avoid obvious temptation. Smokers may find it helpful to read *Packing it in?* (see Further reading). The second stage is to set the scene by getting rid of all the smoking paraphernalia — cigarettes, lighter, matches, ashtrays — and to decide on a date to stop smoking. The third stage is actually stopping; on the day you stop, non-smoking activities such as swimming, a trip to the cinema and visiting non-smoking friends can help to keep the mind off cigarettes. The fourth stage, the hardest for most people, is to keep off cigarettes for good.

If you have decided to stop smoking, you may find it helpful to see your family doctor before you give up, to discuss what you

One of 20,000 entries in the UK nationwide 'Scramble-an-ad' competition for children. The scrambled ads highlighted the risks of smoking. In the process it was hoped the children would be less likely to take up smoking, or be encouraged to give up if they had already started. This poster was by 15-year-old Peter Kong, from Wales.

intend to do. Try not to smoke during the day to begin with. Or you can try delaying the time at which you smoke your first cigarette. The later in the day you start to smoke, the fewer cigarettes you will smoke per hour. It is not that you are smoking fewer just because you are starting later, the frequency of smoking actually decreases.

Many people find it difficult to give up smoking. You may find you lapse and accept one cigarette. The important thing is to keep trying until you succeed. You may experience nicotine withdrawal symptoms, but these normally pass within three to four weeks. These feelings include coughs; headaches; lack of concentration; general feelings of muzziness, tiredness, irritability and anxiety (sometimes so acute you feel as if you are going crazy); trouble in getting to sleep; and weight gain. If you do experience any of these things, remind yourself why you want to kick the habit and remember that they will pass. A few people are fortunate and do not experience withdrawal symptoms.

Some people may be helped in giving up by stop-smoking clinics, which can offer specialist advice.

If you gain weight, which not everyone does, remember you will be much healthier as a non-smoker weighing 5 kg more than a smoker at your present weight, and you will be able to shed the excess weight in the months to come in any case. If your weight worries you, take more exercise: this will help you keep your weight down and make you feel better. If you find you need snacks to make up for cigarettes, then have apples, oranges and other low-calorie foods, rather than chocolate.

> We used to use aversion therapy — or oversmoking — in which we made smokers smoke continuously without let-up until they were sick. It worked, but after 1980 when Nicorette [a nicotine chewing gum] came on the market, we no longer needed to do that. The success rate in our clinics doubled with Nicorette. With this you're getting the nicotine without the harmful effects of the smoke. (Dr Chris Steele.)

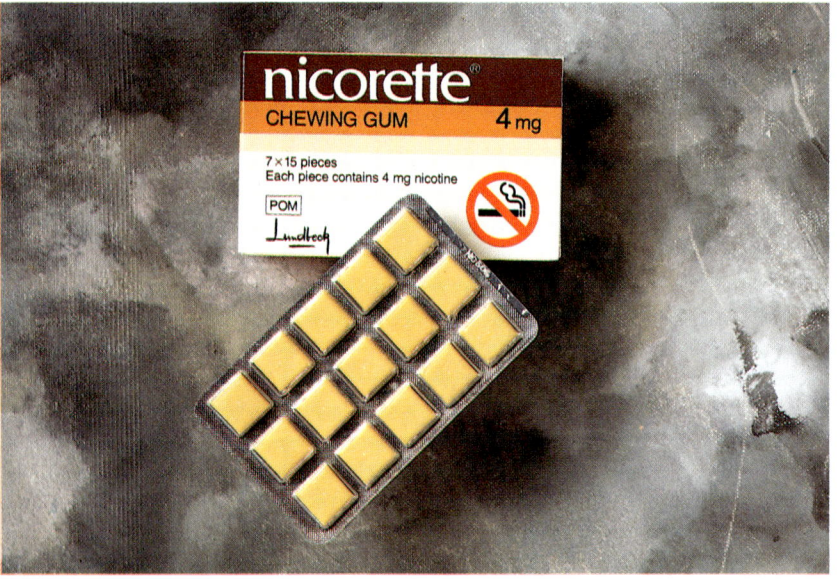

Is nicotine chewing gum safe?

> Nicorette is the only thing that has been shown to be effective in helping smokers give up. It would certainly save lots of lives if people switched from very messy, dirty tobacco to just pure nicotine. They're taking in the nicotine, anyway, in tobacco, so why not just take the nicotine without the other things which cause cancer, heart disease and bronchitis? Even if they become addicted to nicotine gum, that would be nothing like as bad for their health. (Dr Michael Russell.)

---

1 Why do you think governments all over the world have done so little to combat smoking, to introduce non-smoking legislation and to create a smoke-free environment for their citizens?

2 What benefits can someone expect from giving up smoking?

3 How would you help someone who wants to give up smoking but has already failed in two or three attempts?

4 Why do many people find it difficult to stop smoking?

5 Do you smoke? If so, why? If not, what are your main reasons for not smoking?

Nicorette, a chewing gum containing nicotine, is the only aid proven to be effective in alleviating the misery of giving up smoking. Nicorette provides only the comparatively harmless nicotine — saving the former smoker from the dangerous tar and carbon monoxide.

6 The future

Smoking is not just a problem for the developed world. As campaigners there have fought successfully for smoke-free zones and as health education programmes have begun to make an impact, tobacco companies have turned their attention to the developing world. There, as it has been said, 'business is booming'. Between 1986 and 1988, exports by US tobacco companies doubled. The US government has succeeded in breaking tobacco trade barriers in Japan, Taiwan and South Korea. In 1989 it tried to pressure Thailand into opening its market to American cigarette manufacturers. Some people in the USA are angry about this new development.

> At a time when we are pleading with foreign governments to stop the export of cocaine, it is the height of hypocrisy for the United States to export tobacco. (Former US Surgeon General, Dr Everett Koop in *Time*, 2 October, 1989.)

While cigarette consumption in Europe rose by only 5.3 per cent between 1971 and 1981, during the same period it rose by 41.5 per cent in Africa, 31.4 per cent in Latin America and by 28.5 per cent in Asia. This rise in consumption has been supplied by a rise in tobacco production in the developing world.

> In 1970 tobacco production [in Mexico] was 11,000 tons [11,176 tonnes]. For 1980 it was 24,000 tons [24,384 tonnes]. And in 1990 it is estimated at 46,000 tons [46,736 tonnes]. (Dr Federico G Puente Silva.)

Poor people in developing countries, such as here in Ecuador, are tempted by grants from tobacco companies to make a living by growing and harvesting tobacco.

A cigarette factory in the Seychelles. As consumption in developed countries has been going down, the tobacco industry has looked to developing countries to produce and consume more cigarettes.

Why is this?

> ... the growing and selling of tobacco offers many advantages to developing countries, which in the last decade have suffered enormous increases in the cost of imported oil for economic development, severe reductions in the price they can obtain for the basic commodities they export and, latterly, increase in their external debts due to high interest rates imposed by creditor countries. The tobacco companies often give free agricultural advice, credit for fertilizers and seed and a guaranteed price for the finished product, facilities which are frequently lacking for any other crop. Moreover, tobacco taxes offer a ready source of government revenue ...
>
> It is therefore not surprising that short-term needs override concerns about long-term consequences. This leads to some strange contradictions. For example, China has transformed its health-care system in a manner which is enormously beneficial, yet it is the world's largest producer of tobacco. (*Smoking and Pollution: A Teacher's Guide*, Health Education Authority, 1988.)

The future

People in developing countries have enough health problems already, without the additional risks that smoking brings. Poverty, coupled with addiction to nicotine, means that some people have to choose between buying food and buying tobacco:

> Smoking of only five cigarettes a day in a poor household in Bangladesh might lead to a monthly dietary deficit of 8,000 calories. (The Lancet, 16 May, 1981.)

Do the tobacco companies care?

> The average life expectancy here [Burkina Faso] is about forty years, infant mortality is high: the health problems which some say are caused by cigarette smoking just won't figure as a problem here. (Chris Burrell, Rothmans, reported in the Independent Magazine, 29 October, 1988.)

> Unless something is done to combat smoking in Africa, we are going to see a major plague. It is obscene that a major cause of death is pushed on these African countries. (Dr Keith Ball, Consultant Physician, Central Middlesex Hospital, quoted in the Independent, 29 October, 1988.)

While there are more and more smoke-free zones in the developed world, if the people of the developing world are to share in a smoke-free future, they must be given the economic aid to grow crops that will benefit themselves, rather than the powerful tobacco industry.

Below *US Tobacco sales. The price keeps going up, and the sales keep going down. More and more Americans are kicking the habit, leaving tobacco companies no option but to increase the price again and to look for new markets in developing countries where consumption continues to rise.*

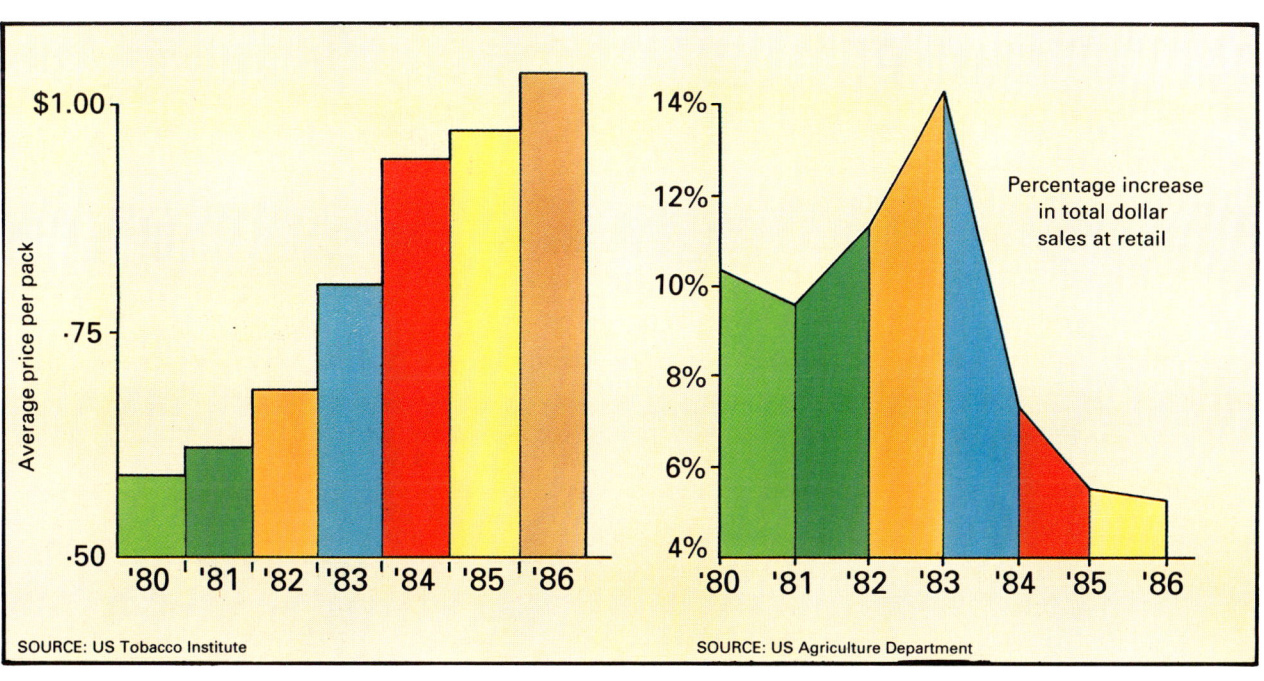

7 Conclusion

Smoking is a problem that affects all of us. This book has looked at important issues surrounding smoking and raised a number of questions. Firstly, we have looked at which groups of people smoke. It has been shown that there are differences in the rate at which certain groups of people are giving up smoking: professional workers are giving up faster than manual workers. The unemployed smoke most of all. Does this mean that health education programmes are failing to convince certain sectors of society? We have also seen that most smokers have their first cigarette during childhood, and how difficult it is to convince children of the dangers of smoking as long as society condones it.

Secondly, the health risks of smoking and passive smoking have been examined, and we have looked at how smoke-free zones can be achieved. Although tobacco companies have been sued for endangering people's health, and although employers can be taken to court for allowing smoking and therefore failing to protect their employees' health, the only way to prevent smoking-related illness is through the creation of a smoke-free environment. This involves helping smokers through stop-smoking programmes.

Thirdly, we have seen that while the campaign to clear the air is succeeding in the developed world, the tobacco companies have turned their attention to the developing world, where they offer economic support to those who grow and sell tobacco. This has resulted in a tremendous rise in tobacco production and consumption. Ultimately, it will result in an increase in smoking-related disease and death for people already struggling to survive.

Finally, we have learnt that there is more to creating a smoke-free world than persuading individual smokers to give up their habit. Employers, shopkeepers, governments and the tobacco industry will all need to play their part:

> There is much for you and me to do. Let us do it together and make a smoke-free society by 2000 a reality that will eliminate a tremendous number of deaths, a great deal of suffering and disability and an economic burden we can no longer bear. (Former US Surgeon General, Dr Everett Koop.)

Below *Dr Everett Koop, US Surgeon General from January 1982 to October 1989, is said to have campaigned so vigorously against smoking and the tobacco companies that the US government could not afford to give him another term in office.*

• Appendix

More girls than boys smoke in the 14–16 age group, but the sex difference evens out later.

Children who smoke
England and Wales
30%
25%
20%
15%
10%
5%
Regular smokers
Boys
Girls
11
12
13
14
15/16
11-16
Age group

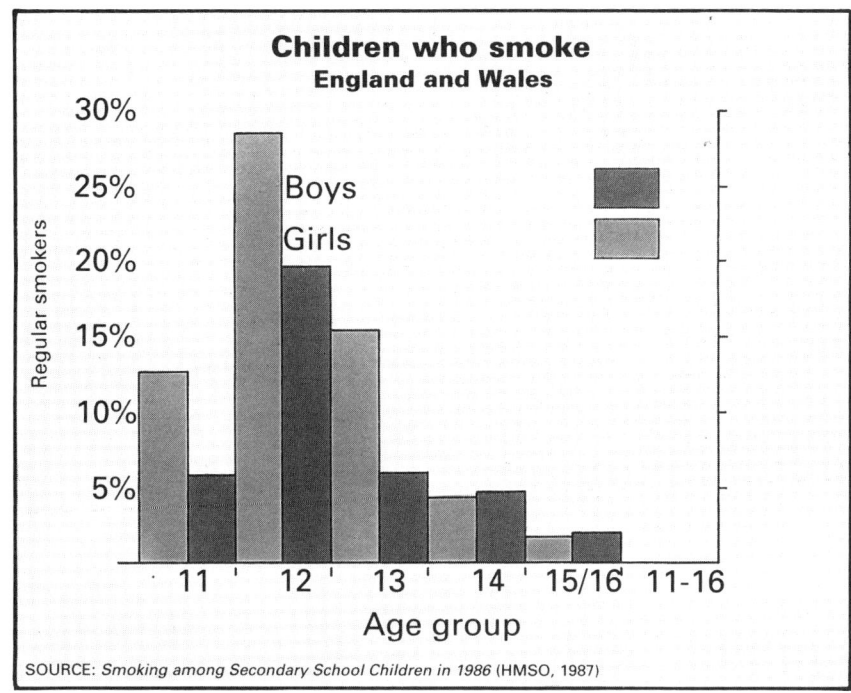

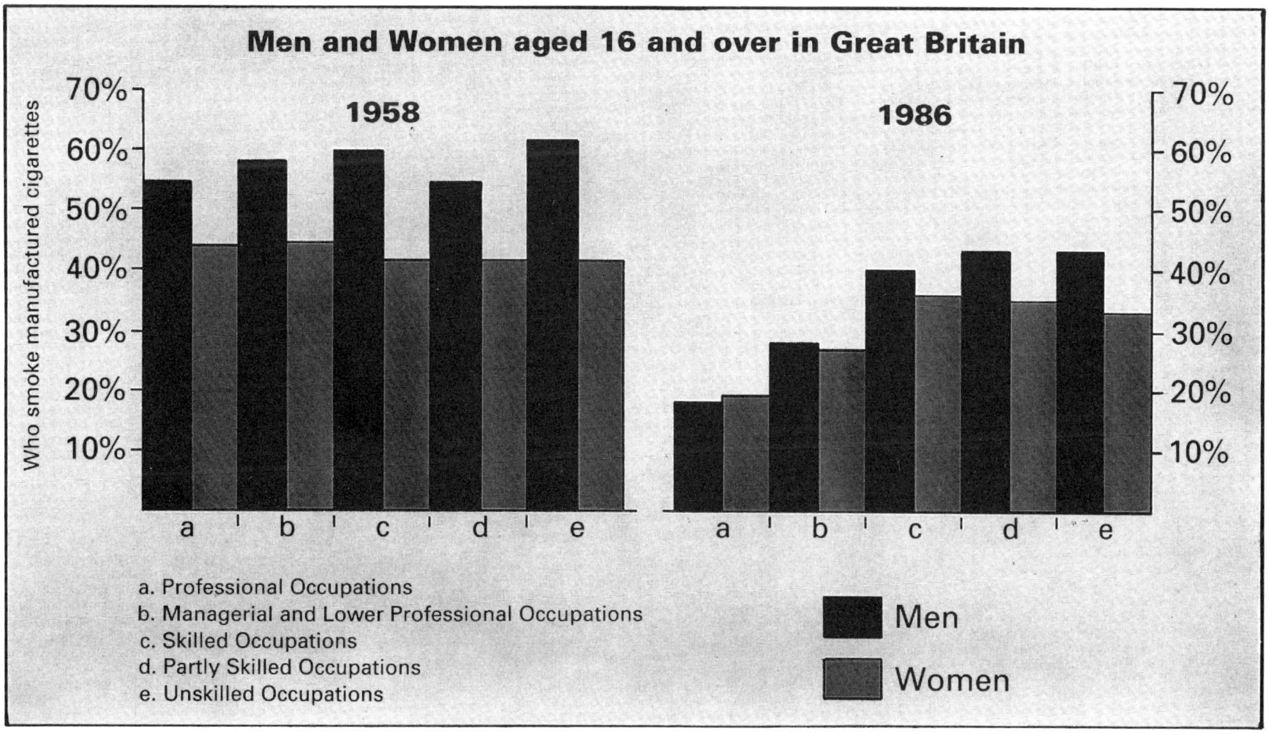

SOURCE: *Smoking among Secondary School Children in 1986* (HMSO, 1987)

Left *It is thought that girls may smoke more than boys in the early and mid-teens because they mature earlier and are therefore going to parties and discos, where they may smoke, earlier than their male peers.*

Below *In adults the sex difference evens out with more men than women smoking. In adults, it is social class that is the significant difference with semi-skilled and unskilled men forming the largest group of smokers. It is said that women find it harder than men to give up smoking, but this is not so. There have never been as many female smokers as male and there are, therefore, fewer to succeed in giving up.*

Men and Women aged 16 and over in Great Britain
1958
1986
70%
60%
50%
40%
30%
20%
10%
Who smoke manufactured cigarettes
a
b
c
d
e
a. Professional Occupations
b. Managerial and Lower Professional Occupations
c. Skilled Occupations
d. Partly Skilled Occupations
e. Unskilled Occupations
Men
Women

Glossary

Anxiety A state of unease or tension.
Behavioural sciences A range of subjects, including psychology, that deal with the study of human behaviour.
Bronchitis Inflammation of the bronchial tubes in the lungs, causing difficulty in breathing.
Carbon monoxide A poisonous gas that is one of the main components of tobacco smoke. It reduces the amount of oxygen carried by the blood.
Carcinogenic Causes cancer.
Carcinoma Cancer.
Creditor country A country that has lent money to another country — usually on condition that the latter pays interest (a percentage of the total amount lent) every year.
Developing country A poorer country which does not yet have the housing, work opportunities, education or health care that rich countries take for granted.
Emphysema Enlargement, and eventual destruction of, the air sacs in the lungs. This leads to an inability to breathe.
Fetus The term for an unborn baby, after the eighth week of pregnancy (before then it is known as the embryo).
Gangrene The death of body tissue because of interrupted blood flow.
Leukaemia Cancer of the white blood cells. These are normally involved in fighting infection.
Median The middle number or the average of the two middle numbers in an ordered sequence of numbers: 7 is the median of both 1, 7, 31 and 2, 5, 9, 16.
Miscarriage The failure of pregnancy before twenty-eight weeks.
Nicotine The addictive substance that is found in tobacco.
Passive/forced smoking Involuntarily breathing in someone else's tobacco smoke.
Peptic ulcer An ulcer is a break in any body surface, internal or external, that heals only with difficulty. A peptic ulcer is one occurring in the stomach or the duodenum.
Pneumonia Inflammation of the lung, which causes fever and sometimes death.
Preventive medicine The prevention of illness and disease, through vaccination, healthy eating and exercise, for example.
Psychiatrist A medical doctor who has been trained to treat mental disorders.
Psychoactive Affecting the mind through chemicals.
Psychologist A person qualified in psychology, which is the study of the mind, how it works, and why people behave as they do.
Stigian Dark, gloomy and hellish.
Tar A thick black sticky substance, found in small particles in tobacco smoke.
Tumour A swelling in the body, especially one made up of an unusual growth of cells.

Further information

You can contact these organizations to find out more about the issues covered in this book.

Australia
Action on Smoking and Health (ASH) PO Box 179, Carlton North, Victoria 3054
Australian Council on Smoking and Health, 42 Ord Street, West Perth, Western Australia 6005
Billboard Utilizing Graffitists Against Unhealthy Promotions (BUGA UP), PO Box 80, Strawberry Hills, NSW 2012
QUIT anti-smoking programme, 12 Victoria Street, Carlton South, Victoria 3053

Canada
Canadian Council on Smoking and Health, 400–1565 Carling Avenue, Ottawa, Ontario, K1Z 8R1
Non-Smoker's Rights Association of Metro Toronto, 344 Bloor Street West, Suite 308 Toronto, Ontario, M5A 3A7

UK
Action on Smoking and Health (ASH), 5–11 Mortimer Street, London W1N 7RH
British Medical Association, BMA House, Tavistock Square, London WC1H 9JP
Cancer Research Campaign, 2 Carlton House Terrace, London SW1Y 5AR
Parents Against Tobacco (PAT), 3 Endsleigh Street, London WC1H 0DD
SmokeQuitters, 363 Wilmslow Road, Fallowfield, Manchester M14 6XU
Smokestop, Department of Psychology, The University, Southampton SO9 5NH

USA

Action on Smoking and Health (ASH), 2013 H Street NW, Washington DC 20006

American Cancer Society, Tower Place, 22nd Floor, 3340 Peachtree Road N.E., Atlanta, Georgia 30026

Americans for Nonsmokers' Rights, American Nonsmokers' Rights Foundation, 2054 University Avenue, Suite 500, Berkeley, California 94704

Tri-agency Tobacco-free America Project (TATFAP), c/o American Cancer Society, 1599 Clifton Road, Atlanta, Georgia 30329

Further reading

Action on Smoking and Health (ASH) *Teenage Girls, and Smoking* (ASH, 1989)

British Medical Association *Smoking out the Barons: the Campaign Against the Tobacco Industry* (John Wiley and Sons, 1986)

Cancer Research Campaign and Teachers' Advisory Council on Alcohol and Drug Education *Packing it in?* (1988) (Stop-smoking package for 15- to 19-year-olds)

Charlton, Dr Anne 'Children's advertisement-awareness related to their views on smoking' in *Health Education Journal vol. 45 no. 2* (1986)

Health Education Authority *Smoking and Me: Pupil's Booklet, A Teacher's Guide and Parent's Leaflet* (Teaching pack for 11- to 13-year-olds) (1988)

Health Education Authority *Smoking and Pollution: Pupil's Booklet, Teacher's Guide, and Parent's Leaflet* (1988)

Jacobson, Dr Bobbie *Beating the Ladykillers: Women and Smoking* (Gollancz, 1988)

Leigh, Vanora *Let's Discuss Smoking* (Wayland, 1986)

Marshal, Alan and Matheson, Jil *Smoking Attitudes and Behaviour* (HMSO, 1983)

Muller, Mike *Tobacco and the Third World: Tomorrow's Epidemic?* (War on Want, 1978)

National Swedish Board for Consumer Policies, National Board of Health and Welfare, and International Organization of Consumers' Unions *Smart Promotion* (1989)

Taylor, Peter *The Smoke Ring: Tobacco, Money and Multinational Politics* (Sphere, 1985)

Ward, Lesley *The Facts About Smoking: A Trainer's Manual* (Health Education Council, 1984)

Wolmar, Christian *Drugs* (Wayland, 1990)

Videos

Confessions of a Simple Surgeon. Promoted by the British Medical Association for use in schools and available from Teltale International, 3 William Street, Edinburgh.

Dr Ricardo and *Seven Ages of Man*. Available, with teaching packs, to schools from Cancer Research Campaign, 2 Carlton House Terrace, London SW1Y 5AR

Acknowledgements

The publishers have attempted to contact all copyright holders of the quotations in this book, and apologize if there have been any oversights.

In addition to those listed in the author's note, the publishers gratefully acknowledge permission from the following to reproduce extracts from copyright material: FOREST:1) Newsletter No.5, January 1982; 2) *The Right to Smoke*, Timothy Evans; the *Guardian*: 1) article by Judy Sadgrove, 7 June, 1989; 2) article by Aileen Ballantyne, 17 July, 1989; Haymarket Magazines Ltd, article in *Autosport*, May 28, 1987; Health Education Authority, *Smoking and Pollution: A Teacher's Guide*,1988; HMSO/Office of Population Censuses and Surveys, *Smoking Attitudes and Behaviour*, 1983; the *Independent*, 29 October, 1988; *International Herald Tribune/New York Times*, 15 June, 1988; the *Lancet*, 16 May, 1981; Sphere, *The Smoke Ring: Tobacco, Money and Multinational Politics*, Peter Taylor, 1985; the *Sydney Morning Herald*, 22 July, 1988; Tavistock Publications, *Smoking: Psychology and Pharmacology*, Heather Ashton and Rob Stepney, 1982.

The publishers would like to thank the following for providing the illustrations in this book: David Bowden 15; Bridgeman Art Library 4, 8; Chapel Studios 25; Eye Ubiquitous *cover*; John Frost 13, 34 (top); Sally and Richard Greenhill 10, 16, 24, 37; Health Education Authority 19, 34 (top), 38; Hutchison Picture Library 5; The Kobal Collection 11; Lundbeck 40; Parents Against Tobacco 30 (Andrew Wiard); Edward Parker 41; Photri 9, 17, 28, 35, 36, 44; St Mary's Hospital 22; Science Photo Library 20; Dr Chris Steele 39; Tobacco Advisory Council 26; Topham 6, 7, 14, 18, 29, 31, 42; *Truth an Ad*/Dick Smith 12, 32, 34, 38; Zefa 27. The artworks on pages 21, 23, 33, 43 and 45 were supplied by Peter Bull.

Index

Page numbers in **bold** refer to illustrations.

addiction to nicotine 7, 15–16
advertising 12–14, **12**, **13**, 30–31, **32**
    Billboard Utilizing Graffitists Against Unhealthy Promotions (BUGA UP) 34, **34**
    sports sponsorship 30–31, **32**
    television advertising 5, 12
Action for Smoking and Health (ASH) 26
Africa
    cigarette consumption 41
Asia
    cigarette consumption 41
    imports of tobacco from USA 41
Australia
    deaths from smoking 5, 35
    non-smoking campaigns 34, **34**
    television advertising 12

British American Tobacco 5

cancer of the lungs 17, 19, 20–21, **20**, 34
children smokers 8, **8**, **9**, 10, 44
    attitudes of 10
    awareness of dangers 28
    effect of adults smoking 10, **10**, 29
    effect of advertising 14
    enjoyment of smoking 14
    tobacco sales to 29–30, **30**
China
    production of tobacco 42
Churchill, Sir Winston **14**
cigar smoking 7, **14**
cigarettes 8–9
    consumption in developing countries 41
    image of sophistication 11, **11**
    sales to children 29
    see smoking
Clarke, Kenneth (UK Health Minister) 33
clean air see smoke-free environment

deaths from smoking 4–5, 34
    statistics 5, **23**

developing countries 5
    cigarette consumption 41
    Ecuador **41**
    Mexico 5, **5**, 41
    tobacco production 42
diseases caused by smoking 17–23, 25
    cancer 17, 19, 20–21, 34

Europe
    cigarette consumption **33**, 41

forced smoking see passive smoking
Freedom Organization for the Right to Enjoy Smoking Tobacco (FOREST) 26

giving up smoking 36–40, **37**, **39**
    motivation 38
    persuasion 36, **36**, **38**
    withdrawal symptoms 39

James I **17**

Koop, Dr Everett (US Surgeon General) 33, 34, 44, **44**

nicotine 19, 46
    addiction 5, 7, 15–16
    effect of on babies 27–8
    psychoactive effects 15
nicotine chewing gum 40
    Nicorette 40, **40**
non-smoking policy 7, 32

Parents Against Tobacco (PAT) **30**
passive smoking 6, 24–5, **24**, **25**, 46
    risks 25, 34
personal freedom 26–7, **26**
pregnancy
    effect of nicotine on 27–9, **27**, **28**

Raleigh, Sir Walter **4**

smoke
    harmful substances in 4, 19–20
smoke-free environment **6**, 29–30, **29**, 32, **35**, 43
smoking
    addiction 7, 15–16

antisocial activity 6
attitudes to 8
dangers **18**, 20–22
effects of **16**, 19, **19**, **20**, **21**, **22**
enjoyment 14, 15
first cigarette 9
government policy towards 5, 32
in public 7, 24, 33
link with poverty **5**, 6
psychological aspects 10, 15
reasons for smoking 8–16
risks of 23
stopping see giving up
tobacco tax 32

tar in tobacco smoke 4, 20, 46
tobacco
    consumption 5, 41, 44
    growing and selling 42
Tobacco Advisory Council (TAC) **26**, 31
tobacco companies 5
    attitudes to advertising 13, 30
    exports to developing world 41–3
    liability for smoker's death 35
    sports sponsorship 12, 30–31, **31**
tobacco plants **7**

UK
    deaths from smoking 5, 17, 19
    smokers 6
    smoking in public places 7, 32
    television advertising 12
USA
    anti-smoking regulations 33–4
    children smokers 8
    Clean Air Act 7, 32
    deaths 5, **23**
    smoking in public 7
    television advertising 12
    tobacco exports to developing world 41
    tobacco sales **43**